# RELIGIONS
## OF THE
# WORLD

## LYNN UNDERWOOD

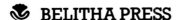 BELITHA PRESS

British Library Cataloguing in Publication Data
CIP data for this book is available from the British
Library

## Acknowledgements

Photographic credits:

Bridgeman Art Library 10, 28/29, 30 right, 40, 42,
    44 top, 45 bottom
The British Library 23 right
Deni Bown 13 left
John Cleare 4
The Anne Frank Foundation/Cosmospress 35 right
Robert Estall 21
ET Archive 46/47
Mary Evans Picture Library 17, 44 bottom, 45 top,
    46 left
Chris Fairclough 56 bottom
Sally and Richard Greenhill 27 right
Robert Harding Picture Library 5 right, 6 right, 7
    left, 9 bottom, 15 top, 26, 33, 35 left, 41, 47 right, 49
Michael Holford 13 right, 15 bottom
Jimmy Holmes 31
Mark Honan 32 left
Hutchison Library 6 left, 7 top and bottom right,
    19 left, 23 left, 27 left, 28 left, 36, 38 left, 50, 53
Magnum 5 left, 12 right, 14, 24, 56 top
Mansell Collection 12 left
Darren Marsh 9 top, 32 right, 51
Susan Mennell 19 right
Network Photographers 30 left, 38/39
Popperfoto 43, 55, 57
Frank Spooner 52
Werner Forman Archive 20 right
Wiener Library 11
ZEFA 20, 48

Illustrated by: Gill Tomblin
Cover illustrated by: Karen Johnson
Chart on p 58-9: Eugene Fleury

Series editor: Neil Champion
Educational consultant: Dr Alistair Ross
Editor: Kate Scarborough
Designed by: Groom and Pickerill
Picture research: Ann Usborne

# Contents

Words found in **bold** are explained
in the glossary on pages 60 and 61

# 1: ABOUT RELIGION

## Learning about Religion

The word 'religion' comes from the Latin *religio,* which means 'respect for what is holy or sacred'. People who do not believe in a religion often find it hard to understand why others do: they may wonder how believers can put their **faith** in something they cannot see or prove by scientific tests. Believers are amazed that anyone can live happily not understanding the unseen powers behind the universe.

### The beginnings of religion

Early man sought to explain the wonders of nature as the work of gods. The miracles of rain, sun and wind were all thought to be the work of gods. People began to gather together to give thanks to these gods and this was the beginning of the formal religions of today.

### How we can learn

It is possible to learn about different religions from the outside by reading about their origins, their history and what their followers

▼ The Sun, the sky, the sea and rain from clouds are all part of nature that seem difficult to understand. It is not surprising that people explained them by making them gods.

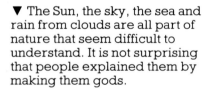

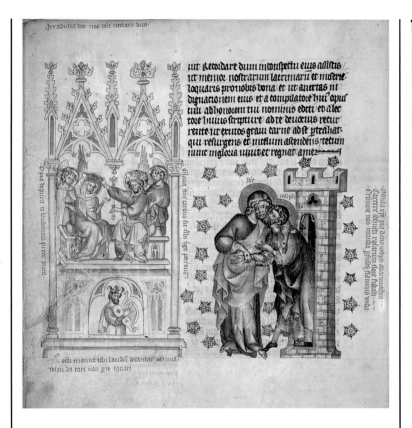

believe. While studying these you will come across the links and similarities between some religions, and also the differences.

You can also learn about religions from people who believe in them. This inside look gives a rather different view. Individuals may not know all the facts about their religion but will have real experience and enthusiasm for their beliefs.

Anyone can learn about religions, find them interesting and move on to other things. To accept a religion as true can mean that people change what they think and what they do.

▲ Two beautifully illustrated religious texts. On the left, the Christian Bible, and on the right, the Muslim Qur'an. The Bible is a copy from the 14th century and the Qur'an, the 18th century.

▼ The symbols used by different religions. These designs identify the religion and its followers.

Christianity

Judaism

Hinduism

Sikhism

Buddhism

Islam

# What is Religion?

▲ Worshippers forming a religious procession outside a Buddhist temple in Burma.

There are many religions in the world today and they are all different. However, they have some things in common that make it possible to compare them.

**God or gods:** most, but not all, religions worship some form of **deity**, a holy being or beings believed to be responsible for the pattern of life on Earth.

**Creation stories:** these are stories that explain in religious terms how the world as we know it came into being.

**Prayer:** all religions expect their followers to spend time either communicating with their god or gods through prayer and ritual or speaking to their own consciences in **meditation**.

**Places of worship:** these are places where people can go to worship their god or gods, pray or meditate and be with other followers. They can be very simple, such as a special place in the wilderness, or very elaborate. They can even be small places in the home that are set aside.

**Priests, ministers, leaders:** people with special responsibilities within organised religions. Their tasks range from speaking to the god or gods on behalf of the followers to offering spiritual and moral guidance to others.

**After-life:** many religions believe that the human spirit lives on after death, either in a special holy place or is **reincarnated** into another life form.

(far left) Muslims praying outside an Islamic mosque in Pakistan. The tall towers on either side of the mosque are called minarets. From these holy men call Muslims to prayer.

◄ A Christian church in St. Vaast-la-Hougue, France. Christian places of worship can vary from small chapels to vast and ornate cathedrals.

**Sacred words or writings:** these are important stories or teachings that provide guidance about what to believe and what to do. Early religions were spread by word of mouth and the exact words were handed down from one generation to the next. Once writing was developed some religions had their sacred words written down. These written words are called scriptures.

**Festivals:** these are special occasions for worship. They may focus on one particular story or aspect of the religion.

**Symbols:** most religions adopt a design that identifies the faith and the worship of that faith.

**Code of life:** all religions set their followers rules by which they should lead their lives. Obeying these rules will, it is hoped, lead to a happy life in this world and any **afterworld** that exists.

▲ A delicately carved Hindu temple in India is a great attraction for Hindu followers.

◄ A rabbi, a Jewish religious leader, preaching inside a synagogue, the Jewish place of worship. Rabbi means teacher in Hebrew.

7

# Forms of Belief

It is too simple to say that religions are divided into those that worship one god or those that worship many gods. Systems of belief are more complicated than that.

## Prophetic religions

Followers of prophetic religions believe in a god or gods that speak to them through prophets or messengers. Followers pray to their god or gods for help and go to their god's messengers for guidance. For example, Judaism is a prophetic religion. Prophets guide the people of the Jewish faith and interpret the will of their God.

## Mystical religions

The followers of **mystical** religions do not believe in gods or holy messengers. They follow a special way of life. Although mystical religions have their wise men, philosophers and enlightened ones, these people are there to help followers find their own way towards wisdom. Confucianism is a mystical religion. Nowadays most of the major religions have aspects of both the prophetic and the mystical.

▶ A Hindu sadhu, or holy man, with some prayer beads and a conch shell, which is sacred to the Hindu god, Vishnu.

8

## An overlap

Particularly in the Far East, the two types of religion overlap. For example, many Buddhists (followers of a mystical religion) also follow prophetic religions (such as Shinto in Japan).

▲ This is a Christian ceremony acting out the suffering of Jesus Christ. According to Christians, his birth and death were foretold by the prophets.

◀ Shinto women priests from Japan. Shinto has successfully combined the prophetic and mystical parts of a religion.

9

# How Religions Spread

▲ St Augustine was a papal missionary who was sent over to Britain by the head of the Christian Church in the late 6th century. He converted the people to Christianity.

People who believe in a religion often share their beliefs with their children. In this way religions can be handed down through the years. Religions can also spread in other ways. Some religions which started as small local beliefs have, thousands of years later, spread all over the world. This has happened for several reasons.

## Migration

First, some religions have spread because people **migrated** from one place to another. They took their religions with them. Sometimes their new neighbours became interested in their beliefs.

Also, when one tribe or nation conquered another, they would often force their religion upon the conquered people.

## Proselytism

Second, religions have spread because believers actively went out to **convert** new followers. This is called proselytism. Both the Christian and Islamic religions, right from their beginnings, have always tried to convert people to their beliefs.

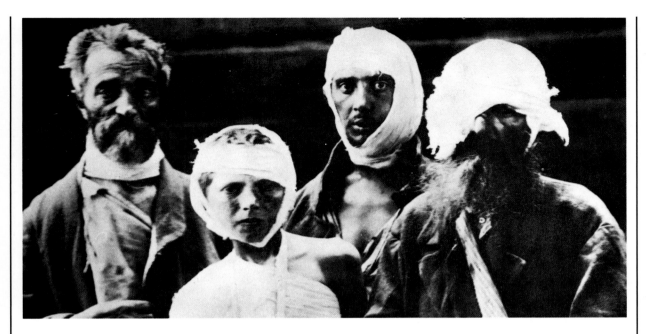

## Seeking

Finally, a religion grows because people seek it. In recent years people have gone out to look for new ideas that would bring some meaning into their lives. Many people from western Europe and North America have made the journey to places like Tibet and India to find out about mystical religions.

▲ The Jewish faith has spread throughout the world. One of the reasons for this is that Jews were attacked in the countries where they were living. This violence forced them to move.

### Medical Missionary

Missionaries are people who set out to convert others to their own religion. They travel to all parts of the Earth to fulfill their mission. They not only take their religion to strange lands but also knowledge of such things as medicine and engineering. David Livingstone (1813-1873), a man more famous for his discovery of the Victoria Falls in Africa, was a medical missionary.

◄ Mystical religions are spreading because people want to follow them. People talk to spiritual leaders and are influenced by them.

# 2: ANCIENT RELIGIONS

## Ancient Gods

▼ Sir James Frazer (1854-1941) spent a large part of his life studying primitive religions and mythology. The results of this study were published in his work, *The Golden Bough*.

The practice of many early religions has died out. They were based on what people thought was important. For example, farmers worshipped gods of the Sun and rain, while warriors worshipped gods of war. Gradually these beliefs were organised into a system of worship.

► Druids were Celtic priests and learned men who taught, organised religious festivals and were skilled in healing. They were stamped out by the Romans in the 1st century AD. However, interest in them revived in the 18th century. Nowadays, amongst other things, druids meet at Stonehenge for the summer **solstice**.

Some ancient religions left a legacy to us in the form of some of their words, their religious art or even some of their beliefs. For example, many superstitions which still exist today come from ancient religions.

## The Norse Gods

Less than 2,000 years ago the religion of the Scandinavian peoples was very common in some parts of Europe. They were a seafaring nation, so their chief god, Thor, controlled the sky, wind and storms. Many stories are told about the Norse gods and their influences are still felt in German- and English-speaking countries. For example, some of the days of the week are named after Norse gods: Wednesday after the god Woden; Thursday after the god Thor; and Friday after the goddess Freya, Thor's wife.

## South American Gods

The practice of some religions died out when the people themselves vanished. The Inca and Mayan civilizations of South America did not survive long when explorers and **colonizers** arrived from Europe in the 16th century. Their religions, which included Sun and animal worship, disappeared with them. Only their great temples and **shrines** remain as evidence that they ever existed.

▼ The Mayan civilization lived for centuries in Mexico and had a highly sophisticated religion. The only evidence left of this religion is found in their art. This is part of a 15th century text showing Mayan gods and nobles.

◄ Mistletoe has many links with ancient North European religions. It was called the golden bough. It is still used in relation to religious festivals like Christmas.

### Did You Know?

The period of the year in which the Christian festival of Christmas falls used to be the Norse celebration of the winter solstice, when the nights were longest. This celebration was called Yuletide, after the Norse god Jolnir (or Odin).

# The Egyptians

The people of ancient Egypt had one of the most advanced of the early civilizations. The remains of it have been found by **archaeologists**. We know a great deal about their religions because so much material about them survives, such as writings and pictures.

## Many Gods

The ancient Egyptians worshipped a whole family of gods. All-powerful was the god Osiris. He was the god of the River Nile, and as the Egyptians could only grow crops along the banks of the Nile (everywhere else being infertile desert) they looked to Osiris and his wife, the goddess Isis, to make their crops grow. There were other gods too, such as Thoth, a bird-headed man, the god of writing and wisdom; and Anubis, a **jackal**-headed man, who was the guide of human **souls** into the next world. The Egyptians built temples for their gods, but only priests and kings were allowed to enter.

## Life After Death

The Egyptians believed firmly in life after death. Their priests would very carefully preserve dead bodies, which would then be wrapped in bandages and placed in elaborate coffins. We call these bodies **mummies**. The mummies of important people were then placed in huge tombs, called **pyramids**, along with all their valuable possessions and some food. The Egyptians believed that the dead person would need these in the next world.

▼ The ancient civilization of Egypt prospered on the banks of the River Nile. This photo shows the Nile as it has been for thousands of years.

▲ The god Osiris, King of the Dead, sits on his throne while Thoth, bird-headed god of wisdom, approaches. This painting is from the Theban Book of the Dead, dated around 1250 BC.

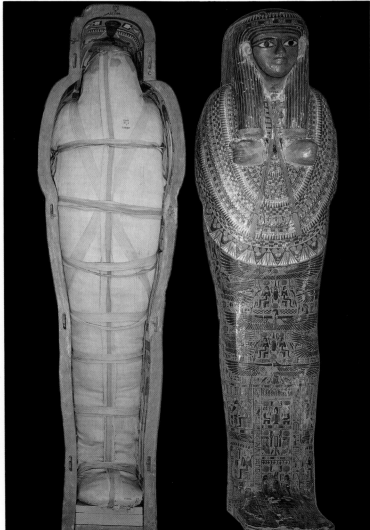

◀ A mummy and the case, called a sarcophagus, of an unknown Egyptian priestess from Thebes. It dates from around 1050 BC.

## The Sumerians

The ancient Sumerians lived in the Middle East between the Tigris and the Euphrates rivers. They worshipped many gods and they also believed in life after death. The afterworld was not a pleasant place. The Sumerians believed that dead people sat in darkness, dressed in feathers and bones and ate earth.

# Greece and Rome

▼ The ancient Greeks and Romans shared a system of belief. Their gods were similar in character but different in name. (From the left) The god of the sea was called Poseidon by the Greeks and Neptune by the Romans. The next two are the most important; Zeus (or Jupiter in Rome) was the father of the gods and mortals and Hera (or Juno) was his wife. Artemis (or Diana) was the goddess of hunting; Aphrodite (or Venus), the goddess of beauty and love; Hermes (or Mercury) the wing-heeled messenger of the gods and lastly Athene/Minerva, the warrior-goddess.

The system of religion the ancient Greeks and, several centuries later the Romans believed in, had influences from places all round the Mediterranean. They believed in many gods, each with control over some natural force, like the sea or land. Poets of the time wrote down the lives and deeds of these gods. These tales are now known as **myths**.

## Greece

The Greek family of gods was headed by Zeus and his wife Hera. Poseidon was the god of the sea, all-important to the Greeks who were a seafaring nation. Demeter was the goddess of the land, who made the crops grow, and Artemis was the goddess of hunting. There were many other gods too.

The Greeks believed that all their gods lived on Mount Olympus in northern Greece, and they built elaborate temples for them. They felt that religion was for all people and so their temples were open to everyone. They thought that every man and woman had a personal relationship with his or her chosen god.

Hera/Juno          Zeus/Jupiter

Poseidon/Neptune

The Greeks also believed that the dead went to a place called the Kingdom of Hades. They reached this place by being rowed across the River Styx by Charon the boatman. It became the practice to place coins on the eyes of a dead body to pay Charon.

## The Romans

About 2,000 years ago, in the reign of the Emperor Augustus, the Romans decided to make their emperor into a god. This was a political move: the vast Roman Empire had so many nationalities and religions in it that the leaders wanted to unite everyone in the worship of the emperor as well as their own gods. In some parts of the empire it was tolerated but in others it caused great unrest. This practice of **deifying** Roman emperors became very common in the Roman Empire.

▲ The Roman emperor, Augustus, who ruled the Roman Empire from 27 BC to AD 14. He was the first emperor to be called a god by his people.

Hermes/Mercury

Aphrodite/Venus

Athene/Minerva

Artemis/Diana

# 3: TRIBAL RELIGIONS

## Religion and Nature

Some cultures exist today that have existed with little change for thousands of years, such as some of the North and South American Indians, the Aborigines of Australia, the Pacific islanders and many different peoples in Africa. They have been able to keep their beliefs because they live in isolated areas.

### Links with Nature

The lives of these peoples depend very much on nature. They hunt wild animals and pick wild plants. Some of them grow crops. The weather affects what they can do and how much food they can get. Their religion is linked to the natural world. They believe that

▼ These are nomadic people who live in the Kalahari desert in Africa. Their tribal religion survives through storytelling.

A ceremonial dance performed by members of a tribe near the Amazon River in South America. Their costumes are made of straw and reeds.

These stone statues are found on Easter Island in the South Pacific Ocean. No one really knows who put them there or why. It is thought that they have religious symbolism.

every animal, every plant, the weather and everything they do, from giving birth to dying, is governed by a god or a **spirit**. Their religions show them how to live in peace with these gods or spirits. Some of them use **magic** that they hope will help them to control events.

## Changes in the Modern World

These traditional religions are passed down by word of mouth from generation to generation: there are stories that parents tell their children and rituals that have to be learned.

In recent years, however, explorers and settlers from other lands have come across these isolated cultures. Often they have upset the traditional way of life and harmed the people. They might have accidentally introduced new diseases or purposefully fought the people to claim their lands. In some cases missionaries from other religions have tried to convert the people. It is difficult for these people to keep their beliefs and customs. However, in spite of the difficulties, some people still uphold their old ways.

A magical symbol used by people in Zaire, Africa, as a charm for casting spells.

# A Way of Life

▲ Totem poles were carved by some Indian tribes of North America and Canada. These poles show the spirits of the animals that the tribe worshipped.

▶ An Inuit (Eskimo) mask worn in religious ceremonies. The face in the centre of the body represents the soul of the Inuit spiritual leader (Shaman).

The religions amongst different communities of people, or tribes, show us a good deal about their way of life. In particular, they show how human beings fit in with the natural world.

## Aborigines

Aborigines in Australia believe that they are part of the land and that the land is part of them. They believe that the land – the rocks, trees and water-holes – contains messages that explain the meaning of life. The land is sacred and must be cared for.

Their religion tells of the creation of the world – **Dreamtime** – when Baiame, the Maker of Many Things, created all life. In the beginning, so the story goes, there were Dreamtime ancestors, who were humans or animals or both. Each person is descended from a particular Dreamtime ancestor and must protect that type of animal as though it were a member of the family.

◀ Images created by the Aborigines in Australia of their Dreamtime ancestors. The kangaroo is considered sacred by certain tribes and the decorated stone is also sacred.

▼ In Peterborough, Canada, there is the largest collection of petroglyphs, or rock carvings, in North America. They were carved between AD 900 and 1400 and are permanent records of traditional Indian spiritual beliefs.

The Aborigines have secret **ceremonies** that teach a way of returning to the Dreamtime. This means that people seek a state of greater understanding in which they can communicate with the natural world around them.

## North American Indians

There are many tribes of North American Indians and they have different traditional religions with different rituals and ceremonies. However, they all teach a deep respect for living things, which they believe to have been made by one creator. Although their way of life depends a great deal on hunting, the people still respect the spirits of all animals. For example, those that hunt deer believe that it is the role of the deer to be hunted for food by human beings. The people, however, should not be too greedy in hunting. Harmony and balance is important because all living things depend on each other.

They also value meditation as a way to be in touch with the spirits of the natural world. There are **medicine men** who heal the sick and keep in close contact with the spirits.

In both the Aboriginal and the North American Indian cultures, the young learn to respect their elders, who teach them their customs and their beliefs.

# 4: RELIGIONS FROM THE FAR EAST

## Buddhism

▼ Young Buddhist monks with begging bowls. These monks have no possessions; they rely on charity for their food and other essentials.

In the 6th century BC Buddhism was founded by Prince Siddhartha Gautama. He lived in Nepal, north of India, and he was born a Hindu. As a prince he lived a life of great luxury. Then, in the space of one day, he saw an old man, a sick man and a dead man. This troubled him, and he left his family and home to think about all the suffering in the world.

He lived for a time in extreme poverty, but hunger and cold made it difficult for him to think, so he decided that one should live a life which took the **middle way** – without luxury or hardship.

After many years of meditation, the Prince claimed that he had discovered the meaning of life and all knowledge came to him. Other people believed him, and he became known as the Buddha, meaning 'The Enlightened One'.

◀ A statue of Buddha in Thailand. There are at least 20,000 Buddhist temples in Thailand.

He travelled the country teaching people how to end suffering and discover enlightenment through the Four Noble Truths. The way to achieve this state is by following the Noble Eightfold Path: right beliefs, right aims, right speech, right conduct, right occupation, right effort, right thinking and right concentration. The Buddha believed that one should strive for wisdom and morality through meditation. He said that if people followed this path they would free their minds from evil, cruelty, deceit and ill-will.

## A Philosophy

Buddhism, as a religion, has no formal structure. It is a way of life or a **philosophy** that allows its followers to believe in other structured religions, such as the Shinto religion of Japan. A person who practises Buddhism must pursue morality; make pilgrimages to sacred places and celebrate holy days and festivals.

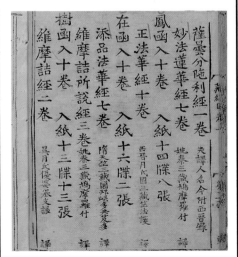

▲ A page from the Tripitaka, the holy books of the Buddhist religion. This copy is Korean and dates from the 11th century.

# Buddhist Sects

▼ A monk tending a Zen Buddhist meditation garden. The patterns in the stones are meant to help clear the mind.

In the third century BC a king called Asoka, who ruled over much of the land that is now called India, sent missionaries abroad to teach the word of Buddha. It was spread throughout the Far Eastern countries and different forms of Buddhism evolved. It became mixed with local religions such as Shinto in Japan and Taoism in China. Some Buddhists began to worship the Buddha as a god, while others simply regarded him as a philosopher and followed his principles, but continued to worship other gods.

There are two main groups of Buddhism. Theravada or Southern Buddhism is quite strict in following the principles set out by the Buddha. This is practised in India, Sri Lanka, Thailand and Burma. Mahayana or Northern Buddhism is not so strict and followed mainly in China, Japan, Tibet and Korea.

These two groups contain many different sects, each with its own particular beliefs. Tibet, for example, has the Red Hats and the

◄ Buddhists often have shrines in their homes. This girl is praying and making an offering of flowers.

▼ The Yellow Hats from Tibet. They belong to a sect of Buddhism that is concerned with personal salvation.

Yellow Hats. The Red Hats are concerned with helping others, while the Yellow Hats are more concerned with personal salvation.

## Buddhism in Japan

Japan is a good example of how many different sects of Buddhism can flourish alongside each other.

There are at least six sects: Tendai, Shingon, Jodo, Jodo Shinshu, Zen and Nichiren are the most prominent. All follow the same basic teachings, they merely differ in their practices. Zen, for example, concentrates on meditation as the route to enlightenment, whereas Shingon expresses itself through many symbols and rituals.

# Confucius and Lao Tzu

▼ A Confucian temple at Qufu, China. Here, followers of Confucius make offerings of food and other gifts to their ancestors. This makes sure that their ancestors are happy in the after-life.

▶ Confucius as a teacher with his followers around him. This is a Chinese painting that has been done on silk.

At approximately the same time as the Buddha was teaching in India, two Chinese teachers were developing ideas that were to become extremely influential.

## K'ung Fu Tzu

K'ung Fu Tzu, or Confucius as he is known, was born in 551 BC in Lu in northern China. He founded a school of philosophy when he was only 22. Many students joined him, but it was only after Confucius's death that his teachings were spread far and wide by his followers.

Confucius believed in order and he believed that this was achieved by having respect for other people and reverence for one's ancestors. It was Confucius who introduced the word Tao, which means 'The Way' or the pursuit of goodness and harmony in life.

Confucians believe in Jen, courtesy and loyalty at all times, and Hsaio, the five relationships in which one had to show these qualities. The five relationships are between father and son; between elder and younger brothers;

▲ A detail from a Taoist temple in Foshan, China.

◀ In many religions, followers believe that people can be taken over by spirits. Some people can act as a go-between for spirits and followers. This is a Taoist spirit medium from Singapore in a trance.

between husband and wife; between elder and younger; and between ruler and subjects. All this was set down by one of Confucius's pupils in books called the *Analects*.

## Lao Tzu

Taoism, said to have been founded by **Lao Tzu** at the same time as Confucianism, is quite different, although the word Tao, 'The Way', is used by both. While Confucius stressed the need to make an effort to maintain order and harmony by following rules, Lao Tzu believed that people should follow **Wu Wei**, which meant that they should be passive and make no effort. The Taoist scriptures are the *Tao Tsang*.

# Hinduism

# THE INDIAN CONTINENT

Three thousand years ago wild Aryan tribes invaded India from the north and settled in the area that is today known as the Punjab. The Aryans had a well-organized religion and regarded their priests as important people in society. A large part of the Aryan religion was the telling of stories and reciting of poems and hymns. Eventually, these were written down in scripture form in Sanskrit. The scriptures are divided into two groups, the Sruti (hearings) and the Smriti (memories). The Sruti contains hymns, poems and prayers, while the Smriti contains stories and laws.

Hinduism is a mixture of Aryan and native religions that were practised in India 3,000 years ago. Today there are more than 400

▲ A Hindu priest, a Brahmin, wading into the River Ganges at Varanasi. This city in the northeast of India is one of the most sacred places in Hinduism.

▶ A lavish illustration from the *Ramayana*, part of the Hindu holy scriptures, which tells of the feats of gods and heroes.

million Hindus throughout the world, mostly in India, and there are thousands of different varieties of Hinduism because it is a flexible religion. Although all Hindus believe in **Brahman**, the absolute force in the universe, they also believe in many lesser **supernatural** beings, which can vary from region to region. There are only a few central Hindu beliefs.

## Reincarnation

All Hindus believe in reincarnation – the idea that the soul passes into another life form upon death – until the soul is released from this cycle. There are three things needed to release the soul; philosophy or knowledge, religious works and devotion to prayer or meditation.

## Caste

Most Hindus who live in India accept a rigid class system called caste. It rules that all people must accept the place in life into which they are born: there is no escape in their current life. However, Hindus generally believe that the principle of **Karma**, or 'deeds', affects their **fate** for the next life.

▲ Some religions have the belief that physical pain helps to purify the soul. This Hindu man from Palni in India has pierced his skin with silver skewers. This purifying of the soul is called mortification of the flesh.

## Gandhi

The caste system allows some people to live very well while others are kept in a lowly position. Mahatma Gandhi played a very important part in leading India to independence from British rule earlier this century. He tried to lessen the worst effects of the caste system by helping the lowest group – the Pariahs or Untouchables, who had to do the dirtiest and most unpleasant jobs. He did such work himself, and called the Pariahs Harijans, which means 'children of God'. ▼

# Hindu Sects

▶ The god Vishnu, in one of his incarnations as Krishna, the wise man, woos a maiden with his flute playing.

▲ A carving from a Hindu temple in India showing the elephant-headed god, Ganesh. He is the god of wisdom and good beginnings and is a symbol of luck and riches.

There are basically three major sects of Hinduism, all of which involve the worship of one of the lesser gods.

## Vishnu

The sect that worships **Vishnu**, the preserver of life, is really divided into 10 smaller sects, because he is a god with 10 different **incarnations**. Each village group or individual worshipper may choose between Matsya the fish, Kurma the tortoise, Varaha the boar, Narasimha the lion-man, Vaman the dwarf, Parasurama the axe-prince, Rama the prince, Krishna the first wise man, Buddha the last wise man or Kalki the wise man of the future.

The Diwali festival, a four-day festival to bring in the Hindu New Year, is in honour of the god Vishnu and his wife Lakshmi, the goddess of prosperity.

## Shiva

Shiva is a god worshipped particularly by the Kashmiris and the Tamils. He is a god with two sides to his nature. Called The Destroyer, he is often depicted as a frightening figure sur-

rounded by evil **demons**. Yet at other times, he is described as a life force and is shown as calm and loving.

▲ A street shrine laden with food in Kathmandu, Nepal. These offerings are in celebration of the Hindu festival, Diwali.

## Shakti

In Bengal and Assam, Shakti, the Mother Goddess, is worshipped. She is a goddess of many faces. Fierce and vengeful, she appears in the form of Kali or Durga as an evil old woman standing on a demon. In her gentle form she appears as a beautiful young woman known as Parvati or Uma. The Dasera Festival, held each year for 10 days at the end of September, is in honour of Shakti's incarnation as the wicked goddess Durga.

### Home Worship

Most Hindu homes have a family shrine, which may just be a corner of a room. The shrine will be dedicated to the particular god that the household worships and there will be a symbol of that god on the shrine.

The worshipper **anoints** the god with perfumed oil while reciting hymns, then lights some joss sticks and sits in front of the shrine to meditate.

Gifts of food or flowers are sometimes placed in front of the shrine.

◄ Women decorating their homes in celebration of the Hindu New Year and the festival of Diwali. Diwali is also known as the 'Festival of Lights'.

# Other Religions from India

Other religions are also practised on the Indian continent, including Islam and Christianity. Three more religions actually have their beginnings in that area and have since spread to other places.

## The Sikhs

The Sikh religion was founded in the 15th century by a teacher, or guru, called **Nanak**. It combines beliefs from both the Muslim and Hindu faiths, with its own distinctive principles. The scriptures of Sikhism are called the *Guru Granth Sahib*.

Sikh children attend a coming of age ceremony which **initiates** them into the Khalsa, the community of the pure. All boys take the name of Singh (lion) and the girls of Kaur (princess). Orthodox Sikh men have to have long hair and beards (kesh), carry a comb (kangha) and a sabre (kirpan), to wear shorts (kacha) and a bangle (kara). The Sikhs regard themselves as warriors.

▲ An Indonesian Hindu cremation ceremony. The dead are placed on wicker platforms and ritually burnt. Hinduism has spread from India to far-off places.

▶ A gathering of Sikhs for a religious ceremony in Bradford, North England. The long beards, sabre and bangle are three of the five features an Orthodox Sikh has to have.

◀ A Jain pilgrim in Western India. He is wearing a mask to prevent him from accidentally swallowing insects.

▼ Parsees see death as a brief victory of evil over good. They take their dead to dakhmas, or towers of silence.

## The Jains

Jainism is a very gentle religion: Jains believe that all life forms have a soul and should not be harmed. Jains will not eat meat and the most **devout** Jains will sweep insects from their path to avoid stepping on them and wear masks to avoid accidentally swallowing insects. Like Hindus they believe in reincarnation but they do not believe in any gods. They believe in an eternal universe and all living things are a part of this universe.

## The Parsees

Parsees take their religion from the ancient **Zoroastrian** religion of Persia (now Iran) which began 2,600 years ago. They believe in one god, **Ahura Mazda**. Life after death is possible for those who live a good and honest life on Earth. A sacred fire is kept burning in their temples at all times. Parsees are not allowed to bury their dead because they believe that death, the work of evil, would **defile** the Earth by burial. Instead they place them on high towers for the vultures to eat.

# 6: JUDAISM

## The History of the Jews

To understand the Jewish faith, one has to know a little about the history of the Jewish people; the two things are impossible to separate.

Nearly 4,000 years ago in Mesopotamia, a man called **Abraham** believed in only one god, **Yahweh**, with whom he made a covenant or bargain. If he and his descendants worshipped and obeyed Yahweh, they would be given the land of Canaan and they would be God's Chosen People. Abraham's descendants became the twelve tribes of Israel.

### The Exodus

The Jews worshipped their one God for many centuries, until a terrible famine came to their land and they were forced to go to neighbouring Egypt for help. The Egyptians made the Jews their slaves, and eventually many of the Jews began to worship Egyptian gods. **Moses** was the next great prophet. He was a Jew who had been adopted as a baby and brought up as

### Passover

Passover is an eight-day festival which celebrates the time when Moses led the Jews out of Egypt. There is a special meal, called the Seder, and a special ritual. The youngest child in the house asks, in Hebrew, 'Why is this night different from all other nights?' The father replies, 'Because we were slaves under Pharaoh in Egypt and God brought us forth out of Egypt.' Then people drink wine and sing psalms of thanks and praise.

The Jews have other festivals to remind them of their history.

▶ Moses, who led the Jews from Egypt, overlooks the promised land of Israel. He never set foot in Israel, dying just before his people reached it.

◄ The Western Wall (sometimes called The Wailing Wall) in Jerusalem is where devout Jewish pilgrims gather to pray.

## The spread of Judaism

Judaism has spread throughout the world from its homeland Israel. Because of migration to Western Europe and then persecution in European countries where Jews had settled, the Jewish faith went with its followers to more distant places. In 1980, there were about 13 million Jews: 5.7 million in the USA, 3.3 million in Israel, 3 million in Europe (including 1.7 million in the USSR) and the rest throughout Africa, Asia and South America.

an Egyptian nobleman. He had a vision from God telling him to lead the Jews out of Egypt and back to the Promised Land of Israel.

This journey was called the Exodus. During the journey, Moses received the laws of Judaism, the **Ten Commandments**, from God and brought the Jews back to their true faith.

## Exile

A few centuries later, Israel was conquered by the Romans, who eventually drove the Jews out. For the next 2,000 years they had to find homes in other countries, although they kept their customs and religion. The Jews were often expelled from countries because of their faith. They were seen as anti-Christian because they do not believe, as Christians do, that Jesus was the Son of God. Many went to newly-discovered lands, such as North America.

In 1948 the state of Israel was established. This has become the official homeland for Jews.

▲ This young Jewish girl, Anne Frank, wrote a diary whilst in hiding with her family in German-occupied Holland during World War II. She described the terrible persecution of the Jews at that time of war.

# The Jewish Religion

▶ The inside of a synagogue with worshippers and a rabbi present. Men and women do not sit together in Orthodox synagogues and all heads are covered as a sign of respect.

## The Creation

The Jewish Scriptures tell a creation story in which God creates the world in six days. The first people, Adam and Eve, are given a garden to live in – the Garden of Eden. An agent of evil appearing in the form of a serpent tempts them to violate God's command. Their act cuts them off from God.

This story is also part of the Christian and Islamic religions.

The Jewish religion is based upon scriptures called the Tenakh. There are 24 books and they are divided into three sections. The Torah lists all the laws that were given to Moses by God and all the rules for the conduct of everyday life. The Nevi'im is the writings of all the prophets of Judaism. The Ketubin contains all the psalms (poems or hymns) written by unknown authors.

## Bar Mitzvah

▶ At the age of 13 all Jewish boys have a coming-of-age ceremony called a Bar Mitzvah when they are accepted as adults in religious events. Some Jews have developed a similar ceremony for girls – the Bat Mitzvah.

## The Role of Scholars

Jewish scholars constantly study the scriptures, sometimes producing different interpretations of Jewish law. These different ways of understanding the law have led to several different sects of Judaism.

Two thousand years ago, Jewish leaders and teachers were given the title rabbi, which means 'teacher'. Rabbis lead religious ceremonies and also give advice and guidance to their people on everyday matters.

## Worship

Jews worship in buildings they call synagogues. The Torah is written on scrolls in Hebrew and each synagogue has a set of these scrolls, which are kept in a holy place in the wall of the synagogue called the **Ark**. At times of worship, the scrolls are brought out of the Ark and carried in procession around the synagogue. Synagogues are designed so that men and women can sit separately.

From sunset on Friday to sunset on Saturday it is the Jewish sabbath, the seventh day of the week. It is a day of rest and worship. Jews may not work on that day and a special ceremonial meal is eaten.

### Kosher Food

The Jewish laws contain rules about what foods can be eaten and how they should be prepared. Although they are religious laws they were medically, quite sensible rules for a country as hot as Israel. Jews do not eat pork or shellfish because these creatures scavenge and can carry disease. Other animals are slaughtered by special butchers who drain all the blood from the carcass before preparing the meat for consumption. Milk must never be drunk when meat is eaten.

▼ The tallith or praying shawl, the menorah, a candlestick with seven branches, and the yarmulka, the skull cap worn by Jewish men, are all symbolic of the Jewish faith.

# Jewish Movements

### Ethiopian Jews

There are black Jews in Ethiopia, many of whom were taken to Israel recently to escape famine. These Ethiopian Jews believe that they are descended from those followers of the **Queen of Sheba**, who converted to the Jewish religion during their time at the court of King Solomon in Israel.

▼ A Liberal Jewish couple celebrate New Year with special food and prayers.

Jewish movements have developed because scholars have interpreted the law in the Torah in different ways.

Orthodox Jews are those people who accept the Jewish laws totally and who follow them strictly in their lives.

Reform Judaism developed in 18th-century Europe. Reform Jews have a more relaxed attitude towards Jewish traditions and rituals and allow women to take a much greater part in the religion. Women are even allowed to become rabbis. Another group, Liberal Judaism, developed out of Reform Judaism.

Conservative Judaism started in the 19th century in America. Conservatives take a middle path: they have less ritual than the Orthodox Jews but still keep to the traditional beliefs.

## Mysticism

Judaism has always had mystical sects in which meditation and contemplation are very important. The Hasidim group is one of these sects. It was formed in eastern Europe in the 18th century. Hasidic Jews show continual religious devotion through prayer.

▲ These are Hasidic Jews, a very strong sect of Orthodox Judaism. They emphasize joy and intensity in their worship. Rather than gathering in large synagogues, Hasidic Jews prefer to pray in small groups.

# 7: CHRISTIANITY

## Christian Origins

The Jews had a prophecy that God would send them a special leader, a **Messiah** who would be born in the town of Bethlehem and who could trace his family back to an ancient Jewish king, David. About 2,000 years ago, according to the writers of the New Testament, Jesus of Nazareth was born and fulfilled all the prophecies of the scriptures.

### The Teachings of Jesus

Jesus grew up a Jew and followed the Jewish faith himself, but he preached an extension of Judaism. Jesus believed that all men and

▼ Jesus, surrounded by his twelve chosen followers, the disciples, at the Last Supper before he was tried and crucified. After the betrayal of Jesus by Judas Iscariot, one of the disciples, the group dropped to eleven. Later they were joined by Paul and the twelve men became known as the Apostles.

## A New Commandment

Jesus said the whole of Jewish Law could be summed up very simply:

'You shall love the Lord your God with all your heart, mind, soul, and strength; and your neighbour as yourself.'

◄ The Sea of Galilee is in the northeast part of present-day Israel. Jesus preached and performed miracles on and around this lake.

## The Trinity

Most Christians believe in God as three parts, a Trinity: God the Father, Jesus Christ the Son and the **Holy Spirit**. These are separate sides of the one God.

women, whether Jewish or **gentile**, should love each other and God with all their hearts. He broke many of the strict Jewish laws by performing miracles, like healing the sick, on a Sabbath (when Jews are not supposed to perform any tasks at all) and by sitting down to eat with non-Jews. He defended people who were cast out by the Jews because they had disobeyed the laws and he preached tolerance of sin and forgiveness of enemies.

His revolutionary ideas caused dismay amongst the Jewish leaders who **denounced** him to the occupying Romans and Jesus was taken into custody, tried and condemned to death by **crucifixion** – a form of execution common at the time.

According to the Gospels, three days after his death he rose from the dead and appeared to his followers. This was called the **Resurrection**. Later, he ascended to heaven.

## The Spread of the Gospel

Jesus's followers began to teach their new religion all over the Roman Empire. They called themselves **apostles**. They said that Jesus had paid the price for people's sin by dying, and that if they believed in him they would enjoy eternal life with him. They called him Christ, meaning 'the anointed one', and the new religion Christianity.

▲ Three symbols for the Christian faith. The fish shape at the top was a very early sign. The Taucross on the left is to remind Christians of the cross Jesus was crucified on and the Chi-rho stands for the first two letters of the Greek word for Christ.

# The Growth of the Church

▶ Groups of men and women formed holy orders; the men as monks and the women as nuns. They live in communities, the monks in monasteries and the nuns in convents. Their role is to devote themselves to God.

▲ An Eastern Orthodox sacred image, or icon, of Mary, the mother of Jesus. This dates from the 17th century and comes from Novogorod, Russia.

At first the Christians who tried to teach other people about their faith were **persecuted** and even put to death in an attempt to stop the growth of this new religion. Much later, the Roman Emperor Constantine was converted, and he made Christianity the official religion of the Roman Empire in AD 313. It was then much easier for missionaries to spread the news of their religion over the empire. The Emperor also called a meeting of Church leaders to discuss the official organization of the Church. They appointed a Church leader called the **Pope** and set up a headquarters in Rome. They also wrote down a statement of belief called the **Nicene Creed**.

## After Rome

When Rome fell into the hands of other peoples, the new conquerors were converted. The next centuries saw many upheavals, and some Christians began to form themselves into special groups to take care of the faith. These

## The Christian Scriptures

The Christian scriptures are called the Bible. They include the Old Testament, which is some of the old Jewish scriptures, and the New Testament. The New Testament includes four accounts of the life of Jesus – the gospels.

There is also a book about the early work of preaching called the *Acts of the Apostles*. Some of the letters written by the apostles are included too, as well as a book called the Revelation, a message from God received in a vision and written down by a man called John. The books were gathered together to make the Bible, as Christians today know it, by about AD 400.

▼ The head of the Roman Catholic Church, the Pope. He lives in the Vatican City which is a separate state within Rome.

groups of men and women, monks and nuns, lived apart and devoted themselves to prayer, teaching and good works – such as providing care for the sick and elderly and safe lodgings for travellers. They also guarded copies of the scriptures and spent many hours producing new copies. In the 12th century AD some people became friars who travelled around teaching and preaching.

## East and West

The Church in the countries to the East kept closely to the old traditions and did not like some of the changes that were happening to the religion in countries to the West. In AD 1054 the Church formally split into two parts. In the West the **Roman Catholic** Church was headed by the Pope in Rome. In the eastern city of Constantinople a leader called the Patriarch headed the **Eastern Orthodox** Church. Both these Churches still practise their own brand of Christianity today.

# CHRISTIANITY

# The Reformers

In the 16th century the Christian Church divided again, into Roman Catholic and Protestant. The Protestant Church believed that the Catholic Church was corrupt and too concerned with ritual, money and politics. As a result of this the divisions of the Church became bitter enemies and fought many wars over their differences in beliefs. This period of Christian history has become known as the Reformation. Because of the pressure on the Catholic Church to change for the better, the 16th century also saw a Counter-Reformation. This movement was the effort made by the Catholics to reform.

## Martin Luther and John Calvin

In 1517 a German monk named Martin Luther openly criticized the Catholic Church. He wrote the Ninety-Five Theses against Indulgences, which were cash payments made to the Church in order to gain forgiveness. He preached that salvation is through faith alone and that the authority of the Bible is supreme over Church laws. The Lutheran church grew rapidly in Germany and Holland.

John Calvin, a French **theologian**, developed his own teachings in 1536. One important difference between his teachings and Luther's was that he said God had **predestined** some people to be saved. His teachings first appeared in France and Switzerland.

## The Spread of Protestantism

During the 16th and 17th centuries, Protestantism spread in many different ways. Groups sprang up, each with separate theories and beliefs. For example, there was a church formed in Switzerland by **Huldreich Zwingli**; the **Huguenots** in France who were followers of Calvin; and the **Presbyterian** church in Scotland founded by John Knox in 1557.

## The Church of England

In England some leaders had already been criticizing the Catholic Church. It so happened

▲ Martin Luther (above) and John Calvin (below), two of the first reformers. ▼

that King Henry VIII wanted a marriage **annulment** from his Spanish wife, Queen Catherine, and the Pope (who was under the influence of the Queen's nephew, the **Holy Roman Emperor** Charles) would not allow it. This provided Henry with the perfect excuse to break away from the Church of Rome and set up the Church of England. This move allowed the king to take for himself all the lands and power that the Catholic Church had in England. The Anglican Church which developed remained very similar to Roman Catholicism until the spread of Protestantism and its sects.

## Religious Conflict

Throughout Europe at this time, there was a great deal of unrest and religious intolerance was largely to blame. For example the zealous Spanish Catholics formed a special court called the Inquisition which tried those who would not conform to Catholicism. During the reign of Elizabeth I, a Protestant, many Catholics were executed. The fighting was not just between Catholic and Protestant; Protestant fought Protestant for religious supremacy.

▲ Thomas Cranmer, Archbishop of Canterbury, helped King Henry VIII organize the Church of England.

▼ In the 17th century the Catholic Church in Spain set up the Inquisition. This court tried those who rejected Catholicism. If they did not conform, they were called heretics and burnt at the stake.

# Christians in the New World

▶ The departure of Puritans from Delft in Holland in 1620 to join the *Mayflower* and sail to the New World.

▲ John Wesley (1703-91) was an English preacher who set up a new Protestant group called the Methodists. This church is now widespread in the USA.

In the 16th and 17th centuries, just as new religions were gathering followers, the lands of North and South America were being discovered. Among the people who decided to go to these new lands and settle there were those who found that their beliefs were not well accepted in their own countries. Some of the first to travel to North America were 102 English **Puritans** who crossed the Atlantic Ocean in the ship the *Mayflower*. This religious movement has had a lasting effect on religions and society in the USA. Today North America has many different forms of Christianity.

## Revivalism
In the years after the Reformation up until now there have been several outbreaks of intense

## Living Simply

The Amish, Mennonites and Hutterites are all groups of Christian sects that developed in the European Reformation. They insist on a simple life-style and live together in a community of sharing with one another. They are still found all over the world, but they are best known in the United States and Canada, where their 'horse-and-buggy' lifestyle contrasts with the frantic race for wealth in the rest of society. They are recognized as excellent farmers, and they are generous in giving any extra money they have to help the needy.

religious excitement, mainly within the Protestant beliefs. These outbreaks are known as revivals. For example, in the 18th century, John Wesley set up a group called the Methodists, who were taught to believe in salvation by faith alone. They had **lay** preachers. They were separate from the Anglican Church and are now most widespread in the USA.

## Billy Graham

The latest revival is being led by Billy Graham, an American **evangelist**, who has used television and radio to get across his message. He also holds large public meetings, not only in America, but all over the world. The word evangel means gospel. So an evangelist is someone who looks to the gospels for truth.

▲ An Amish couple in their horse and buggy. As part of their religion, these people have rarely accepted or used modern technology. They prefer to live in the simplest way possible.

# 8: ISLAM

## The Prophet Muhammad

The Islamic faith was proclaimed by the Prophet Muhammad, who was born in the city of Mecca in AD 571. Mecca is in present-day Saudi Arabia. As a young man he helped in his uncle's business. On trading trips to the north he probably met and talked with many Christians.

When Muhammad was about 40, he developed the habit of going off into the hills to think and contemplate. He was disgusted with the various religions that were practised in Mecca which he considered corrupt. He claimed that God, whom he called Allah, had told him to denounce these other religions and to preach a return to worshipping the one true God.

Muhammad could not read or write, but he dictated Allah's words, which he said were

▼ Pilgrims gathering at Mecca, the most holy city of Islam. The Prophet Muhammad was born here.

◄ Muslims in Pakistan kneeling on prayer mats that face towards Mecca. They are called to prayer by an official of their mosque, called a muezzin, five times a day.

## Reading the Qur'an

▲ The Qur'an has 114 chapters (*suras*). It contains many instructions to Muslims on how to worship, how to treat their fellow human beings, what to eat and wear and general rules about family life.

## Ramadan

The Muslims have several important festivals each year. Ramadan lasts for a whole month, and during the festival every Muslim over the age of 10 fasts between sunrise and sunset. Muhammad felt that this gave Muslims self-discipline. At the end of Ramadan they celebrate the Night of Power, when Muhammad received his first revelation.

given to him by the Angel Gabriel, to his Companion, a follower known as Abu Bakhr. These words formed the Qur'an, the holy book of the Islamic faith.

Followers of Muhammad became known as Muslims. They believe that he was the last of the great prophets of God – the prophets of the Jews and Christians. One very important difference was the place of Jesus: he was seen only as a great prophet.

# ISLAM

# How Islam Has Spread

▼ These tiles, decorated with Islamic script, come from a mosque in Isfahan, Iran. There are no images of creatures or people in mosques as Muslims believe they would compete with Allah.

▶ The Muslims spread the word of Islam throughout the Mediterranean. Evidence of their conquests are still seen in Spain for example. The architecture of this building is typically Muslim.

Islam first grew largely by war and conquest. Muhammad was a warrior prophet who believed that it was a duty to wage a holy war, a jihad, on the enemies of Islam.

Muhammad's first conquest was his own city. In AD 622 he left Mecca with his Companions for the city of Medina. This was the great emigration, or hijra, which marks the start of the Muslim calendar today. He gathered together the people of Medina and attacked Mecca, which finally surrendered. Muhammad got rid of the various religions there and also sent the Jews away, because they would not follow the Islamic faith. He **dedicated** the ancient sanctuary of the Kaaba in Mecca to Allah.

By the time of Muhammad's death in AD 632 most of the people in the country followed the Muslim faith. His place as leader was taken by rulers called **caliphs**. The first four were chosen from his band of Companions, but the

line continued afterwards. A hundred years later, the caliphs had created an Islamic Empire which covered parts of India, North Africa and Spain. They had done so by fighting many wars, and they were fearsome in battle.

In the 13th and 14th centuries the Islamic Empire spread further into India, China and Mongolia. Then in the 15th century it spread into eastern Europe.

During the 15th century the Spanish drove the Muslims from the Spanish mainland. The private armies of Europe, who had been fighting the wars known as the **Crusades** against the Muslims for many years without great success, finally succeeded in capturing the holy city of Jerusalem. They rededicated it to the Christian religion. Gradually the empire grew smaller, due to poor leaders from Mecca and rebellion in the occupied countries. However, even when countries freed themselves from the political rule of Islam, there were numbers of people who kept the Islamic religion.

In recent years there has been a rebirth of Islam in some of the Arab countries and elsewhere.

▲ Every year, the Spanish on the south coast of Spain act out the Muslim invasions of the 15th century.

## Jinn

The Qur'an tells of the existence of angels and also of jinn, or genies, who are spirits created from fire and who serve God. Wicked jinn are called demons and their chief is Satan, sometimes called Iblis. God allows Satan to tempt people and to test them.

Many of the folk tales from Islam are tales of jinn who can grant wishes or perform magic feats.

# Islamic Sects

► The ayatollah is the leader of the sect of Shi'ite Muslims. An ayatollah can pass laws based on his understanding of the Qur'an. This can give him great powers.

## The Five Pillars of Islam

**Shahada** The basic statement of faith is 'There is no God but God and no prophet but Muhammad'.

**Salat** Prayers must be said facing Mecca at sunrise, noon, mid-afternoon, sunset and night.

**Ramadan** Muslims must not eat, drink or smoke between sunrise and sunset in the month of Ramadan.

**Zakat** Muslims must give about $2\frac{1}{2}$ per cent of their income and some other types of property to charity.

**Hajj** A Muslim, if physically and financially able, must make the journey to Mecca at least once.

There are two main groups within the Islamic faith – the Sunnis and the Shi'ites. They accept all the teachings of the Islamic faith, the Five Pillars of Belief and the Qur'an. They differ on the importance of the leaders after Muhammad.

## Sunnis

The Sunnis believe that after Muhammad the caliphs were simply elected leaders. They follow the teachings of only the first four caliphs after Muhammad's death. About 80 per cent of Muslims are Sunnis.

## Shi'ites

The Shi'ites believe that Muhammad's true successor was his nephew, Ali, and that his descendants possess secret knowledge and have a special place as holy men or leaders.

They call these men Imams.

The important religious leaders among the Shi'ite sects are called mujtahids (inter-preters). They have great authority and they preach a **fundamental** belief in the Qur'an as it is written. Mujtahids are sometimes called mullahs or ayatollahs and some claim to be descended from Muhammad.

▲ Strict Muslim women dress in a chador, which is a piece of cloth that covers them from head to toe. Only their eyes can be seen.

## Ahmadis

Another group within Islam was founded at the beginning of this century by Mirza Ghulam Ahmad, who lived in India. He claimed to be a prophet. Unlike the other groups, he rejected the idea of the jihad, or holy war, and it seems that he wanted to unite all religions under Islam. Ahmadis have made numbers of converts in the West and in Africa.

# 9: RELIGIONS TODAY

## New Beliefs

Throughout history there have been new religions and new sects that have developed. Some have lasted a long time while others have disappeared quickly. Today this process is still happening.

### New Sects
Sects are developed within a religion when some believers try to change ideas that they think other people have got wrong. For example, they may say that certain activities, such as drinking alcohol or wearing certain types of clothes, are or are not allowed.

### New Religions
From time to time people develop entirely new religions that meet their needs for meaning and purpose in life. The Rastafarian religion was developed in the Caribbean. It is based in part on some ideas from the Bible but

▼ (left) A family of Rastafarians. There are many different types of Rastafarians but, in general, they believe that God is in all men and that black people are especially favoured.

▶ (right) Hari Krishna followers in the West are influenced by Hinduism from the East. They shave their heads and sing and dance through the streets.

says that the Ethiopian emperor, Ras Tafari, was the Messiah. This faith has a special message for black people: a belief that they will go back to their homeland in Ethiopia.

The Baha'i faith developed in Persia, now Iran, in the 19th century. It says that all the world's great prophets or spiritual leaders, including Abraham, Moses, Jesus, Muhammad, Buddha, Krishna, and Zoroaster were all used by the One God to teach people. Baha'is seek

▲ The symbol for the Baha'i faith which originated as a split from Islam. Its founders were viewed as imams or messengers from God.

◄ Members of the Unification Church founded by the Korean Sun Myung Moon in 1954. They are holding pictures of their absent partners in a mass wedding.

peace and unity with others. Ironically, Baha'is in Iran are persecuted.

In modern times several sects have arisen out of the Hindu traditions in India. The **Hare Krishna** movement, whose followers shave their heads and wear long orange robes like Buddhist monks, is one that has survived a number of years.

## Jehovah's Witnesses

Charles Taze Russell (1852-1916) from Pittsburgh, USA, founded this sect. Witnesses reject the idea of the Trinity and follow the teachings of the Bible exactly. They actively try to convert others to their way of thinking.

## Cults

A cult is a breakaway movement from established religions which is often led by a charismatic leader who has specific, sometimes bizarre, ideas about religion. Many cults attract people who are searching for something new – a new lifestyle. Some cults are harmless but others have caused great distress to the families of their followers because cult leaders have encouraged followers to break off all communication with relatives and devote themselves entirely to the cult. Many cults offer followers very little. The followers often live in great hardship and poverty, giving all their money to the cult. Unfortunately, several cults have been exposed as frauds, where the sole purpose was merely to make the leader of the cult very rich, at the expense of his or her followers.

# Living Together

▶ Mahatma Gandhi, a spiritual and political leader in India, who tried to get Hindus and Muslims to live peacefully together.

## Multiculturalism

Countries that include people from different nationalities are **multicultural**. The leaders of the country can decide either to encourage people to change to fit in with the existing culture or find ways to encourage them to keep their own culture. For example, they can allow children to follow the religion their parents want to teach them and let people have time off work when they need it for their own religious festivals.

New forms of travel have changed the world a great deal. People know about new places or go to live in them more than ever before. This movement of people means that more is known about other religions.

In many countries there are people who belong to different sects and different religions. An important question is how people with different beliefs can live together.

▶ A Christian church found in Simla, north India, which is largely Hindu, is a strengthening sign of different religions being able to exist together.

◄ Bob Geldof, through the power of rock music, managed to raise millions of pounds for the starving in Africa. This is an example of how charity spans all faiths.

▼ Mother Theresa from Calcutta works amongst the poor and sick people of India. She has been seen as an example of dedication to the well-being of other people.

## Two Poles

On the one hand there are some people who will not tolerate any beliefs other than their own. Some people will even isolate themselves from the rest of society so that they can follow a set of beliefs their own way. Other people with a rigid set of beliefs try to force those around them to think and act in their way. There can be conflict as a result.

Still, it is important to remember that people who seem intolerant usually believe very deeply that what they are doing is right. It is important to find out why they think this way before judging them.

On the other hand, some other people and countries tolerate all kinds of beliefs. This tolerance happens when people understand and respect other people's beliefs.

## Agnosticism

An agnostic is a person who confesses, honestly, that he or she just does not know whether to believe in the existence of a god or not. Agnostics would have to be convinced but would *like* to believe.

According to research done by the Vatican, there are about 819 million agnostics in the world.

# Time Chart

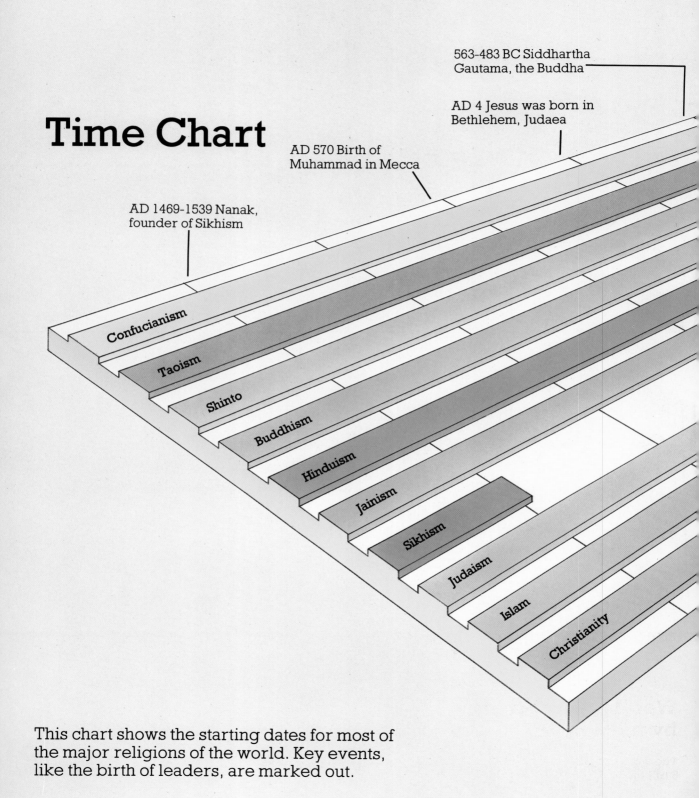

563-483 BC Siddhartha Gautama, the Buddha

AD 4 Jesus was born in Bethlehem, Judaea

AD 570 Birth of Muhammad in Mecca

AD 1469-1539 Nanak, founder of Sikhism

Confucianism

Taoism

Shinto

Buddhism

Hinduism

Jainism

Sikhism

Judaism

Islam

Christianity

This chart shows the starting dates for most of the major religions of the world. Key events, like the birth of leaders, are marked out.

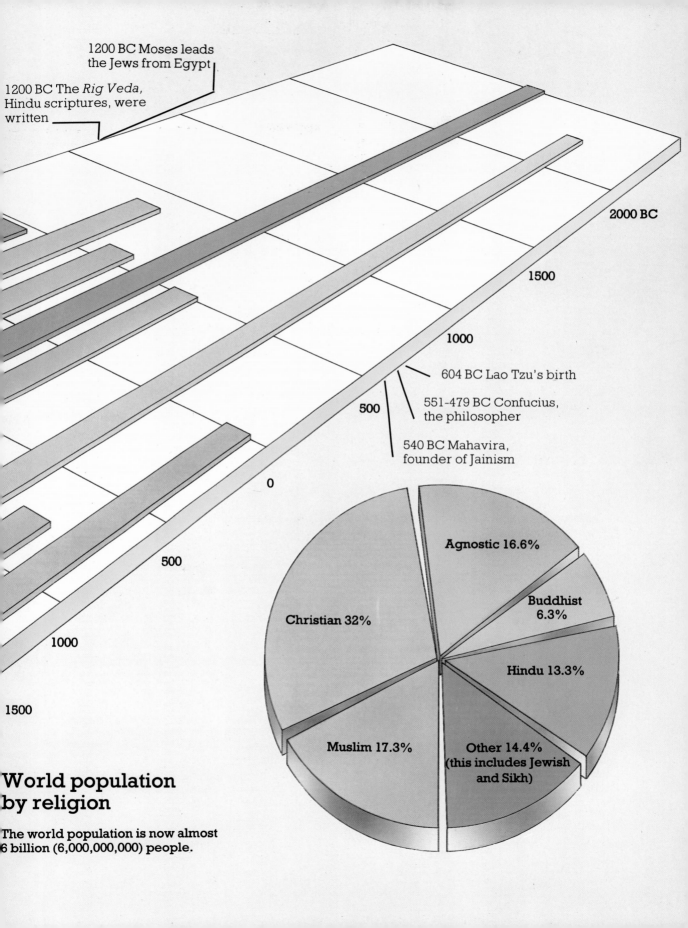

1200 BC Moses leads
the Jews from Egypt

1200 BC The *Rig Veda*,
Hindu scriptures, were
written

2000 BC

1500

1000

604 BC Lao Tzu's birth

551-479 BC Confucius,
the philosopher

540 BC Mahavira,
founder of Jainism

500

0

500

1000

1500

Agnostic 16.6%

Buddhist
6.3%

Christian 32%

Hindu 13.3%

Muslim 17.3%

Other 14.4%
(this includes Jewish
and Sikh)

# World population
# by religion

**The world population is now almost
6 billion (6,000,000,000) people.**

# Glossary

**Abraham:** the first well-known Biblical figure of the Jewish faith. He is regarded as a holy man by Christians and Muslims as well.

**afterworld:** the places where the souls of the dead go.

**Ahura Mazda:** the **Zoroastrian** name for God. It means 'wise lord'.

**annulment:** this is like a divorce but means for the Catholic Church that two people were never married. So each partner is free to marry again.

**anoint:** to apply oil to a person or an object as a sign of respect and reverence.

**apostle:** one of the twelve men chosen by Jesus to preach his message to the world.

**archaeologist:** a person who studies history through the remains of ancient cultures.

**Ark (of the Covenant):** the sacred container for the laws of the Jewish people.

**Brahman:** the absolute or the divine in Hinduism. Brahman is in all the gods and in everything that exists.

**caliphs:** the titles of the successors of the Prophet Muhammad. They are the rulers of Islam.

**ceremony:** a formal act or ritual meant to mark a special occasion.

**colonizers:** people who settle in a new land and make it their home.

**convert:** to persuade someone to change their beliefs.

**crucifixion:** an ancient form of punishment. A person was nailed to a wooden stake or cross and left to die.

**Crusade:** a holy war engaged in by medieval Christians against Muslims.

**dedicate:** to devote a person or an object to a religious cause.

**defile:** this word means to make dirty or to corrupt.

**deify:** to raise to the status of a god.

**deity:** this is a word for a god or goddess.

**demon:** an evil spirit or devil.

**denounce:** this word means to condemn strongly or to inform against.

**devout:** a word used to describe someone who is deeply religious.

**Dreamtime:** the time when, according to Australian aboriginal culture, the world was created by **supernatural** beings.

**Eastern Orthodox:** a branch of the Christian Church dominant in Eastern Europe, Greece and Turkey.

**evangelist:** a Protestant who preaches to others to persuade them to believe in God.

**faith:** an unquestioning belief in something.

**fate:** some people believe that events in their life are controlled by a guiding force. This is called fate.

**fundamentalism:** a strong belief in the truth of religious writings. The people who are fundamentalists follow exactly the teachings of their religion as they see them.

**gentile:** anyone who is not Jewish.

**Hare Krishna:** a recently formed sect of Hinduism whose followers are mainly people from the West (Europe and the USA).

**Holy Roman Emperor:** the name given to Charlemagne in AD 800 and his successors. They were German kings who brought most of Europe under their rule, with the blessing of the Pope.

**Holy Spirit:** Christians believe that God is in three parts – the Father, the Son (Jesus) and the Holy Spirit (the unseen part of the Christian God that is always present).

**Huguenots:** these people were French Protestants of the 17th century. They were greatly influenced by Calvin, but became unpopular in France and were driven out.

**incarnation:** when a god or person takes the form of a human body, the body is known as an incarnation. This word especially describes the form the Christian God took, Jesus.

**initiate:** this word means to introduce someone as a new member of a religious group.

**jackal:** a dog-like animal found in Africa.

**karma:** a Sanskrit word which explains, to those who believe in **reincarnation**, how the events in your present life are the result of actions in a past life.

**Lao Tzu:** the founder of the mystical religion, Taoism. He is said to have been a famous philosopher and was meant to have written the *Tao de jing,* the main text of Taoism in the first century BC.

**lay:** a person who is not an official priest or religious leader, but who plays an active role in preaching.

**magic:** an art that performs acts that are difficult or impossible to explain by any natural means.

**medicine man:** a person in certain tribes, believed to have **supernatural** powers.

**meditation:** this word describes the act of thinking deeply, especially on religious matters. It can also mean the emptying of the mind of all thought.

**Messiah:** a Hebrew word meaning someone who has been sent by God to free a nation and lead them according to God's will.

**middle way:** the way, according to the Buddha, to reach perfection. It is the right path between comfort and hardship.

**migrate:** to go from one place and settle in another.

**Moses:** the man who is regarded as the father of Judaism. He received from God the Laws on which the religion is based.

**multicultural:** a number of different cultures living together in one region or country.

**mummy:** a body that has been wrapped in bandages and preserved so that it never fully decays.

**mystical:** this word is used to describe those things in religion that are difficult to understand and explain, yet at the same time they are essential to that religion.

**myth:** a story about events or people in the past that cannot be proved to be true.

**Nanak:** the founder of the Sikh religion. He lived from 1469-1539 and wrote many hymns which form part of the Sikh manuscripts.

**Nicene Creed:** in AD 325 the Christian bishops met at Nicaea in present-day Turkey and devised a statement of belief for the Church, a creed.

**persecute:** to treat people badly because of their race or religion.

**philosophy:** this word comes from Greek and translated it means 'lover of wisdom'. In a religious sense it means the beliefs and values that people live their lives by.

**Pope:** the head of the Catholic Church world-wide.

**predestination:** the belief that events in a person's life are fixed and controlled and that these events are unchangeable.

**Presbyterian:** a branch of the Christian Protestant Church, influenced by Calvin, which is mainly English-speaking.

**Puritan:** a Christian Protestant movement of the 16th and 17th centuries. The movement wished to purify the Church of unnecessary ceremony and decoration.

**pyramid:** a giant and complicated tomb built for ancient Egyptian kings and queens.

**Queen of Sheba:** also known as Balkis. Her story appears in the Bible and the Qur'an. She visited King Solomon from her country, Ethiopia, and took back with her his religion as well as his child, so the legend goes.

**reincarnated:** this word means to be reborn.

**Resurrection:** a rising from the dead or a revival to life. Christians believe that Jesus rose from the dead and this is known as his Resurrection.

**Roman Catholic:** this is one of the oldest branches of the Christian Church and is headed by the **Pope**.

**Sanskrit:** an ancient language that is no longer spoken. Hindu scriptures are written in Sanskrit.

**shrine:** a holy place dedicated to a god or gods where their followers worship privately.

**solstice:** the time when the Sun is the greatest distance from the Equator. It is considered the height of Summer.

**soul:** this word is used to describe all the vital and essential characteristics that are part of one person. These are seen as a separate being from that person's physical body. Most religions hold the belief that the soul lives on after the death of the body.

**spirit:** this is a being without a body. A spirit is much the same as a **soul**, but does not necessarily come from a physical being as a soul does.

**supernatural:** something that is beyond natural explanation.

**Ten Commandments:** the original ten laws given to Moses by God on Mount Sinai. These form the basis of the Jewish and Christian religions.

**theologian:** a person who makes a study of religion.

**Vishnu:** one of the three main gods of the Hindu religion, the others being Brahma and Shiva. He has many different forms.

**Wu Wei:** the way as described by **Lao Tzu**, the founder of Taoism. It means to accept and be passive, not to attempt to change things.

**Yahweh:** the sacred name of the God of Israel is unpronounceable. It is YHWH. This gave rise over the centuries to Yahweh and, eventually, Jehovah.

**Zoroastrianism:** the religion of the followers of the Persian prophet, Zoroaster who lived around 1400 BC. Little is known of the early religion, but after the 6th century BC it became the state religion of three Persian empires. It still survives to this day, but the number of followers is small.

**Zwingli, Huldreich:** a Swiss Protestant reformer (1484-1531). Originally he was a Roman Catholic priest, but embraced the Protestant movement under the influence of Martin Luther.

# Index

A **Bold** number shows the entry is illustrated on that page. The same page often has writing about the entry too.